ontents

Two cities of Vesuvius

The coast of Italy south of Naples is a popular holiday destination. Every summer tourists flock to resorts like Sorrento, Positano, and Amalfi and the beaches are packed. 3000 years ago this area – known as Campania – was already attracting visitors, and, in the 8th century BC, merchants from Greece set up trading posts in two small villages called Pompeii and Herculaneum.

Pompeii was on a river close to the sea. Boats carried goods between its harbour and ports around the Mediterranean. It soon became an important centre for trade. Herculaneum was a smaller settlement used by traders from nearby Neapolis (Naples). Both towns were prosperous and attracted the attention of invaders. They were occupied first by the Etruscans, and then by the Samnites, fierce warriors from the mountains inland.

But an even more powerful enemy was looking greedily at this rich and fertile area. 220 kilometres north of Pompeii was the city and **republic** of Rome. In the middle of the 4th century BC the Romans invaded Campania. Between 310 and 302BC they captured both Pompeii and Herculaneum.

The Italian coast south of Naples

4

John and Elizabeth Seely

Heinemann

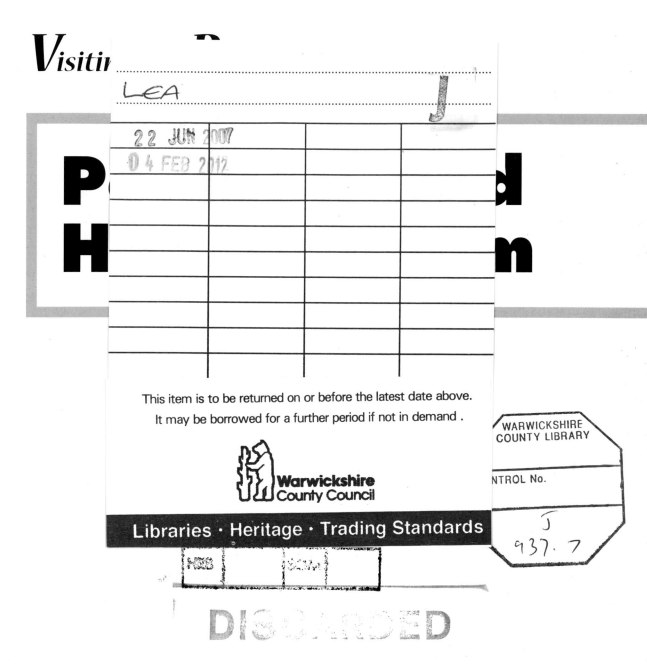

www.heinemann.co.uk
Visit our website to find out more information about **Heinemann Library** books.

To order:
☎ Phone 44 (0) 1865 888066
▤ Send a fax to 44 (0) 1865 314091
▢ Visit the Heinemann Bookshop at www.heinemann.co.uk to browse our catalogue and order online.

First published in Great Britain by Heinemann Library,
Halley Court, Jordan Hill, Oxford OX2 8EJ,
a division of Reed Educational and Professional Publishing Ltd.
Heinemann is a registered trademark of Reed Educational & Professional Publishing Limited.

OXFORD MELBOURNE AUCKLAND JOHANNESBURG BLANTYRE GABORONE
IBADAN PORTSMOUTH NH (USA) CHICAGO

Designed by Visual Image
Illustrations by Visual Image
Printed in Hong Kong

ISBN 0 431 02770 6 (hardback)   ISBN 0 431 02777 3 (paperback)
03 02 01 00 99   04 03 02 01 00
10 9 8 7 6 5 4 3 2 1   10 9 8 7 6 5 4 3 2 1

British Library Cataloguing in Publication Data

Seely, John
    Pompeii and Herculaneum. – (Visiting the past)
    1. Pompeii (Extinct city) – Juvenile literature
    2. Herculaneum (Extinct city) – Juvenile literature – 3. Italy –
    Antiquities – Juvenile literature
    I. Title II. Seely, Elizabeth
    937.7

Acknowledgements

The Publishers would like to thank John Seely for permission to reproduce all photographs.

Cover photograph reproduced with permission of Robert Harding Picture Library.

The Publishers would like to thank Joe Scott for his comments in the preparation of this title.

Every effort has been made to contact copyright holders of any material reproduced in this book. Any omissions will be rectified in subsequent printings if notice is given to the Publisher.

Any words appearing in the text in bold, **like this**, are explained in the Glossary.

Growing prosperity

For nearly four centuries the two towns grew and became prosperous. Wealthy citizens from Neapolis liked to have a seaside house at Herculaneum, while Pompeii remained an important trading post. It became a centre for many different industries, including the making of woollen cloth.

The Bay of Naples and Mt Vesuvius

Judging by its size, and the houses that have been excavated, by AD62 Pompeii probably had a population of about 20,000: a large town by the standards of the time. It was home to businessmen, lawyers and doctors, working families, shopkeepers and slaves. But in that year something happened which threatened to change the lives of the inhabitants of both towns forever. This is how it was described by Seneca, a writer of the time:

'Pompeii, the famous city in Campania, has been laid low by an earthquake. A flock of hundreds of sheep was killed, statues were cracked and some people were so shocked that they wandered about as if deprived of their wits.'

A married couple from Pompeii. They are believed to be the lawyer Terentius Neo and his wife.

In the shadow of the volcano

The reason for the destruction of AD62 faced the citizens of Pompeii and Herculaneum every morning when they got up. Immediately to the north towers Mount Vesuvius, an active volcano. It is one of a chain of volcanoes that stretches down the Italian coast as far as Sicily and the famous peaks of Stromboli and Etna.

In the year 62 Vesuvius rumbled and heaved, but did not erupt. People set about rebuilding their shattered towns. They made rapid progress and life soon returned to normal. But worse was to follow. Seventeen years later, early on the morning of 24 August AD79, the people of Pompeii felt the earth shake violently beneath them and then, as they looked towards Vesuvius, the mountain exploded. Flames leaped into the sky followed by an umbrella cloud of poisonous smoke. Not long afterwards pieces of red-hot rock and dense clouds of ash began to cascade down on the town.

The ash was thick and formed a layer which quickly rose up the sides of the houses. There was panic. Some people tried to hide inside their houses, while others ran out of the town towards the sea. But the ash and the poisonous fumes were deadly. From the remains that have been found it is estimated that at least 2000 people, one-tenth of the population, were killed.

While the rest tried to escape, the ash and rocks continued to fall, until the whole of Pompeii was buried under a layer four or five metres deep. The ash covered everything: houses, gardens, animals and people.

Everywhere in Pompeii, you are aware of Vesuvius looming above the town.

Herculaneum's fate

Herculaneum escaped the ash and the rocks, only to suffer a different fate. The eruption threw up huge jets of steam which reached temperatures approaching 1000° Celsius. As the steam cooled, it turned into boiling rain which mixed with the ash and rocks that had already fallen, to make a river of boiling mud which flowed down the mountain side and covered the city. Most of the people had already fled, but a few had stayed and were killed by the avalanche. When the mud cooled it turned into solid rock – up to eighteen metres deep!

This painting from Pompeii shows Bacchus, the god of wine, and Vesuvius, which is planted with vines.

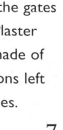

Terrified, people tried to escape from the eruption. This man and child were overcome and died near one of the gates of Pompeii. Plaster casts were made of the impressions left by their bodies.

The buried cities

Immediately after the eruption, the Roman authorities helped the survivors find new homes. There were some attempts to rescue valuables from Pompeii – as is shown by graffiti scratched on the ruins. But there was nothing that could be done to rescue the two cities and they remained hidden for over 1500 years.

The remains of Pompeii were discovered by accident in 1594, but they were not systematically excavated until the 18th century. Even then people were more interested in finding and taking away statues, **mosaics** and other beautiful objects than in trying to understand the lives of the people who had lived in the city. Gradually, however, **archaeologists** uncovered the city and began to realize just what a wonderful historical record lay beneath their feet.

Herculaneum was much more difficult to excavate than Pompeii, because of the great depth of solid rock that covered it. Also, a modern town now stands over much of the site. So even today only a small part of the Roman town has been excavated.

Frozen in time

Pompeii provides us with a fascinating picture of town life during the 1st century AD. Today it is possible to visit the site and stroll round the streets, just as if you were in a modern town. You can go into houses and shops that look much the same as they must have done nearly 2000 years ago. Some of the houses still have the beautiful paintings and mosaics that decorated then when Vesuvius erupted. In the wine shops you can still see the jars that were filled with wine and, in the bakery, the grain mills and bread ovens remain undamaged. In one bakery archaeologists even found charred loaves that were being baked.

The site of Pompeii is about 1200 metres long by 700 metres wide. It was a planned town with many of the streets forming a regular grid, based on two main streets. The Via dell'Abbondanza ran from east to west and the Via Stabiana ran from north to south. (All the names given to streets and buildings are modern ones, usually in Italian; we no longer know what the original names were.) In the south-west corner of the town were the great **forum** and the main public buildings. The rest of the town spread out to the east and the north.

A street in Herculaneum. Many of the houses are in a very good state, protected for centuries by the volcanic rock.

A street in Pompeii. In the distance you can see Vesuvius.

The town centre

Most people who visit Pompeii today arrive first at the **forum**. This was the great open square where people would meet to talk and go about their business. The forum was very big: over 150 metres long and nearly 40 metres wide. It was the equivalent of a modern town centre, although in fact it was at one end of the town.

The forum at Pompeii. The building on the right is the Temple of Jupiter, the most important religious building in the town. The white columns at the far end are the remains of the **colonnade** and gallery that surrounded the forum on three sides. These columns carried a roofed and shaded walkway so that people could shelter from the sun in summer and the rain in winter. (In mid summer, temperatures regularly rise above 30°Celsius.)

Around the forum

At the far end of the forum, are the remains of the offices of the **duovirii** and the **aediles**. The duovirii, or magistrates, were the two most important officials and were elected each year to administer justice. The aediles were responsible for the streets, sanitation, the markets and the games. There was also an office for the members of the town council.

Around the sides of the forum were other temples and important public buildings. One of these was the **basilica** (we know this, because someone scratched the word 'basilica' on one of the walls before it was destroyed by the earthquake of AD62). This was a great hall, based on the main halls of the private houses of wealthy men. It was used as a meeting place for businessmen and lawyers. Law cases were discussed and decided and business deals were arranged. At other times the basilica was used for meetings and other social events.

The basilica was a large building with tall columns, like this one (below), which many believe supported a heavy timber roof to protect people from the weather.

Near the Temple of Jupiter was the **macellum** (above). Although Pompeii was full of shops selling all kinds of produce, the macellum was the main food market where all manner of fruit, vegetables and meat could be bought. It also housed a large fish market and a place for changing money.

Earning a living

Pompeii was the centre of a prosperous farming area famed for its cattle, which produced abundant milk, and sheep, which provided wool to be made into cloth. So the town had many shops selling local food, drink and manufactured goods. But it had started as a centre for international trade and remained one under the Romans. So goods from many different countries found their way into its shops too. Pottery was imported from France and when **archaeologists** excavated the town they found a whole crate of French pottery waiting to be unpacked.

The main commercial area ran along the Via dell'Abbondanza. Here you would find not only bars and restaurants, but also shops and workshops. Often a building would contain a workshop, a shop and living quarters for the owner and his family. The manufacture of woollen cloth was particularly important.

Verecundus' shop in the Via dell'Abbondanza

The fullonica of Stephanus: the new cloth was placed in large vats like this one and treated with soda, **potash**, **fuller's earth** and human urine. (Stephanus even placed a large jar outside his shop and invited passing men to help fill it!)

Working with cloth

Wool was brought into the town and processed by craftsmen like Stephanus and Verecundus. After the wool had been spun and woven into cloth it had to be cleaned and dyed. Stephanus owned a large workshop, called a **fullonica**, where new cloth was washed. After cleaning, the cloth was dyed, using vegetable dyes. The fullonica was also used as a laundry for dirty clothes.

Across the road was the workshop and shop where Verecundus made and sold felt for blankets, hats and slippers. He was clearly a successful businessman and had large pictures painted on the outside of his shop to advertise his wares.

Other trades in the town included perfume-making, carpentry, plumbing and wheel-making. There were also several bakeries.

The bakery of Modestus: you can still see the large, stone mills which were used to grind the corn. They were in two parts: the lower half was a large cone-shaped stone. A hollow stone, shaped to fit, rested on it and the grain was poured in at the top. As the top stone was turned (using slave and donkey power) the grain was ground between the two stones and came out at the bottom as wholemeal flour. After the flour had been made into dough, the circular, flat loaves were baked in a brick oven.

Eating and drinking

Food and drink were very important to the people of Pompeii. Despite the violence of the eruption that buried the town, the remains of many different foods were found in shops and homes. Food shops sold fruit and vegetables, dried goods like beans and chickpeas, meat, fish, cereals, milk and wine.

The vineyards on the slopes of Vesuvius produced good white wine, Vesuvium, which may have been similar to the wine Lacrima Christi for which the area is famous today. Wine was made at farms and villas near Pompeii, and sold by the town's wine merchants. If you wanted to have a drink, you could go to a bar like the **thermopolium** of Asellina. Food was also on sale and some bars offered live entertainment, provided by dancing girls. Customers also used to pass the time in gambling games.

This shop in Herculaneum sold cereals and wine.

Fruit grows well around Pompeii. This painting shows pomegranates, which still grow in the gardens there.

Local speciality

Pompeii was also famous for the making of a special fish sauce, called **garum**. This was highly prized by the Romans and widely used in cooking, as we know from many writers of the time. It was made from sardines and other small fish. The fish were gutted and the guts were mixed in a vat with chopped fish and eggs and then pounded to produce a pulp. The vats were left in the sun for several weeks so that the mixture fermented and some of the liquid evaporated. Then the pulp was strained and the liquid used as a sauce. Not surprisingly the factories where garum was made produced a smell that not everyone found pleasant – the writer Seneca complained bitterly about it!

The thermopolium of Asellina had a long marble counter with circular holes in it. These were to hold the amphorae – long jars which had bases that were pointed rather than flat. In summer the wine was served cool, but in winter people preferred it hot.

As you might expect in a town near the sea, fish was a popular food and wealthy people spent a lot of money on large and expensive fish. This **mosaic** shows some of the fish that could be caught in the sea near Pompeii.

The city streets

As you wander around Pompeii, it is strange to think that you are walking along the same pavements and streets as people did over 2000 years ago. The roads are paved with slabs of grey, volcanic rock from Vesuvius – just like the streets of nearby Naples today. The pavements were a lot higher than the level of the road – for a very good reason. Not only did the road act as a drain for rain-water, but it also carried away a lot of rubbish and even sewage. This made it rather unpleasant to cross, so there were stepping stones to help people keep their feet clean. (In Herculaneum there was a sewerage system that ran under the streets, so there was no need for stepping stones.)

The stepping stones were arranged with gaps so that the wheels of carts could pass through. We know that the streets of Pompeii carried a lot of wheeled traffic, because there are deep grooves where the wheels have worn away the stone. In Herculaneum, on the other hand, there seems to have been little wheeled traffic, which is probably because it was much less of a manufacturing and trading centre than Pompeii.

A street in Pompeii with stepping stones so that people could cross the road without getting their feet wet.

A manhole cover in Herculaneum leading to the sewer under the road.

A good water supply is very important to any city and Pompeii had excellent water. It was piped from springs in the hills and fed into large, raised tanks. From these it was carried through lead pipes to the larger houses and also to fountains which were placed at regular intervals along the streets. Many of these were carved with the heads of humans or animals.

These wheel ruts show how many carts must have used this road in Pompeii.

A fountain in Herculaneum. It is carved with the head of the god Neptune.

17

Beautiful homes

Many of the ordinary working people of Pompeii lived in small houses like those on the Via dell'Abbondanza, but both Pompeii and Herculaneum are also full of large and beautiful houses. They have given **archaeologists** and historians a very detailed picture of how people lived and how the shape and design of houses changed during the towns' history.

The houses were very different from what we are used to. The larger houses had very few windows looking out into the street. Instead they were built around one or more courtyards or gardens and daylight came into the house from these. In a typical house you entered from the street into an open space, the **atrium**.

Many houses had impressive doorways, like this one at Herculaneum.

The atrium was usually partly roofed, but in the centre it was open to the sky to allow in light – and rain. Beneath the opening a stone tank, called the **impluvium**, collected the water.

Around the atrium were small rooms, including bedrooms, and often a larger room, which was used as a dining-room, called the **triclinium**. Kitchen arrangements were often very primitive. The kitchen was a small room, often only big enough for one slave to work in, and contained a sink and a brick oven. There was no chimney and the smoke just went out through a hole in the roof. This was not only unpleasant, because the kitchen filled with smoke, it was also dangerous and many house fires were caused in this way.

Cooking utensils from a house in Pompeii

The windows of the rooms did not usually have glass, so, at night and when the weather was bad, they were closed with shutters. This made the rooms dark and stuffy. The only light was provided by naked flames – tapers, candles or lamps. It takes 100 candles to give the same light as one modern light bulb, so it is not surprising that there are many descriptions of how people who spent a lot of time reading suffered serious eye problems.

The family often placed the shrine to their household gods, called the **lararium**, in or near the atrium. This is the lararium of a wealthy Pompeii family, the Vettii.

19

Beautiful gardens

The Romans loved gardens and many of the larger houses at Pompeii and Herculaneum had large, enclosed gardens. From the **atrium** you would pass through another doorway into a larger open space surrounded by an open veranda supported by columns. This was known as the **peristyle**.

Archaeologists have discovered a lot about the trees, shrubs and plants that these gardens contained. There were fruit trees: pears, figs and pomegranates, as well as vines trained over **pergolas**. Roses flourished, and in the spring there were violets and hyacinths. Some houses also had a vegetable garden. We know from writers of the time that people grew lettuces, peas and sprouts.

Loreius Tiburtinus, who owned this house (right), was a priest of the Temple of Isis. The followers of this goddess believed that water symbolized life, so he had a stream running through the centre of his garden with a carved fountain in the centre.

The peristyle formed an enclosed garden surrounded by rooms (left), which opened on to it. This is the garden of the House of the Painted Venus. It is called that because of the paintings on the wall at the back.

Running water

As you might expect in a country that was very hot in summer, people liked to have water features in their gardens: little streams, fountains and man-made waterfalls. Other decorations included marble statues and **sundials**.

The House of Neptune and Amphitrite at Herculaneum. This beautifully decorated inner courtyard was used for meals in the summer.

Many house owners liked to continue their gardens into their houses by having garden paintings on the walls. These paintings can give us a very vivid idea of what their gardens were like. This painting is from the House of the Painted Venus.

Having a good time

The citizens of Pompeii liked to enjoy themselves. They were enthusiastic theatre-goers, so it is not surprising that there were two theatres in the town. The large theatre was probably built in about 200BC. Like many theatres in Greece, where theatre had first developed, it was built on a slope and looked out towards open countryside, which provided a natural background for the plays.

Smaller performances of plays, mimes, music and recitations took place in the Odeon, the small theatre. This was built over a hundred years after the large theatre and could accommodate about 1000 people.

This **mosaic** of musicians shows a scene from a comedy.

The large theatre at Pompeii seated up to 5000 people, who came to see Greek and Roman tragedies and comedies. Plays took place in daylight.

Dangerous games

Romans liked the theatre, but they loved watching fighting even more. At about the same time as the Odeon was built, work started on a huge **amphitheatre**. Here the people of Pompeii went to watch the **gladiators**. These were slaves and prisoners of war who had been trained as professional fighters. In the amphitheatre many different types of combat were staged: fights on horseback, fights with swords and **tridents**, and encounters between gladiators and wild animals, including bulls, wild boar or even bears. (One of the graffiti in the amphitheatre announces: 'Felix will fight bears'.) These were fights to the death: when one gladiator had another at his mercy he would turn to the magistrates in charge of the games to ask whether he should kill him or not. Sometimes the decision was left to the crowd. The animals were not shown any mercy.

The amphitheatre at Pompeii was large enough, some people think, to seat the entire population. The whole building was 140 metres by 105 metres and the arena is nearly 70 metres long. Because the theatre had no roof, an awning was put up to shade the audience. (There are graffiti advertising the games which announce: 'There will be awnings'.)

The games at the amphitheatre were as popular as football matches are today – and sometimes there was trouble on the terraces. This painting from Pompeii shows a riot in the amphitheatre between the people of Pompeii and visiting fans from Nuceria. It happened in AD59; several Nucerians were killed and the games were banned for ten years.

The body beautiful

Another cruel sport the people of Pompeii enjoyed was **cock-fighting**. This took place not at the **amphitheatre**, but at the **palaestrum** nearby. Not that the palaestrum was built mainly for blood sports, it was really a huge, open-air sports centre, where the young men of the town went to train for sports and to keep fit. The young men were encouraged to be well-behaved and disciplined by the formation of the Augustan Youth Movement, which organized games and athletics competitions as well as horseback parades through the town.

Cock-fighting attracted gamblers. In this **mosaic** you can see the bag of money that has been bet on the fight.

Visiting the baths

Hygiene, too, was very important. Some of the larger houses had their own bathrooms, but many did not. The city provided a number of public bathhouses which were open from noon until late in the evening. Any citizen could use them and they were very popular. In some there were separate sections for men and women. If there were not, then men and women had different times allocated to them.

The palaestrum at Pompeii where the young men prepared for a variety of athletic events and other games, and used the large swimming pool you can see on the right. Like a modern pool, it had a shallow end and a deep end.

When you went to the baths the first room you came to was a dressing-room, called the **apodyterium**; then you went through a series of rooms, each one warmer than the last. The first was the **frigidarium**, or cold room. From there you passed through the **tepidarium** and on to the **caldarium**, the hot room. Here there was a hot bath, in which bathers could immerse themselves, and a cold basin to cool the bathers down again. People didn't use soap; instead they had oil, soda and body scrapers.

People didn't just go to the baths to get clean; they went to meet friends, have a chat and catch up on the latest gossip. There were people selling food and drink, and most bathers took at least one slave to help them, so the rooms must have been very crowded.

The apodyterium of the women's baths at Herculaneum (above). It is decorated with a large mosaic and has shelves for the bathers' clothes.

The caldarium of the women's baths at Herculaneum.

Personal beliefs

The Romans believed in many different gods, most of whom they had taken over from Greek religion. Probably the god most frequently mentioned and depicted in Pompeii was Venus, the goddess of love and the mother of all nature. She is referred to in graffiti scrawled on walls, especially by young men who felt that they had been badly treated by their girlfriends. Verecundus the felt-maker had a picture of Venus on the wall outside his shop, and one wealthy family had a large painting of Venus, arising from the sea, on their garden wall.

All these gods were worshipped in their temples. They were part of the 'official' religion of the Roman Empire. But many people in Pompeii wanted a more personal religion that would give their lives meaning and hope, so they turned to what are called 'mystery' religions.

One of the Greek gods the Romans adopted was Apollo, the god of peace and truth, whose temple and statue were on one side of the **forum**.

On special occasions animals were sacrificed to the gods. In this carving the priests prepare for a sacrifice.

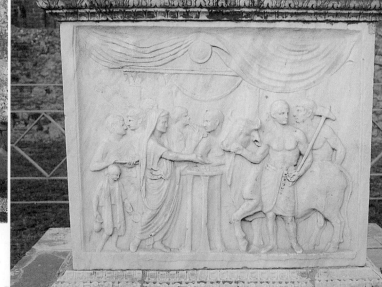

The cult of Isis

One of the most popular was the worship of Isis, the Egyptian goddess of fertility, wife and sister of Osiris, the god of the Underworld (where people went when they died), and the judge of the dead. The followers of Isis believed that if they lived their lives in the right way and attended the services at her temple, they would be rewarded by life after death. Paintings and other evidence from the Temple of Isis at Pompeii have told us a lot about this cult.

Such beliefs were very important, especially since people's lives were so short: medical science was primitive and many did not live much beyond 40 years of age. People prepared for death by planning and paying for large and elaborate tombs. As one comic writer of the time said: 'It makes no sense to decorate the house you live in now, but not the one where you'll spend so much longer.'

Tombs were built outside the city walls (right). These are near the Nucerian Gate at Pompeii.

The Temple of Isis was open every day. The climax of the day's worship was the afternoon service of the blessing and offering of water, the source of all life, shown in this painting (left).

27

Timeline

8th century BC	Greeks establish a trading post at Pompeii and a settlement at Herculaneum, probably on the sites of earlier villages
c.520BC–c.425BC	Campania, the area around Pompeii and Herculaneum, is invaded first by the Etruscans and then by the Samnites
c.425BC–c.350BC	Period of peace and prosperity, under Samnite rule
c.343BC	Romans begin their invasion of Campania
310BC–302BC	Pompeii and Herculaneum are occupied by the Romans. Both towns are made 'allied cities' which means that they can use their own language, control their own trade and elect their own magistrates.
2nd century BC	The **forum** is laid out as we see it today. Temple of Jupiter, **basilica** and large theatre are built.
91BC	Pompeii and Herculaneum join the rebellion against Rome. Both cities are besieged by Sulla and conquered.
80BC	Pompeii is placed under the direct rule of Rome. A lot of Romans move to the city and settle there. Sulla's nephew Publius Sulla becomes the city's leading citizen and 'patron'. Many new buildings are put up and the city grows in size and wealth. Buildings in Pompeii that date from this period include the forum baths, the **amphitheatre** and the Odeon. (Herculaneum does not grow at the same rate because Romans do not settle there in the same numbers.)
73BC	The area around Herculaneum is threatened by the rebellion of **gladiators**, led by Spartacus. They defeat the Roman army but are eventually overcome and killed.
AD59	The riot in the amphitheatre at Pompeii. In heavy fighting between Pompeians and people from Nuceria, several Nucerians are killed. The games are banned for ten years.
AD62	An earthquake badly damages both cities. Rebuilding begins immediately.
AD79	The eruption of Vesuvius destroys Pompeii and Herculaneum
AD1594–1600	The site of Pompeii is discovered by the Italian architect Domenico Fontana, while cutting a channel to divert the course of the River Sarno. There is no serious attempt to explore the site.

AD1709	The ruins of Herculaneum are discovered under the property of the Prince of Elboeuf, while a well is being dug. Excavation reveals marbles and sculptures.
AD1738	The excavation of Herculaneum begins on the orders of Charles of Bourbon, King of Naples
AD1748	Charles orders the excavation of Pompeii

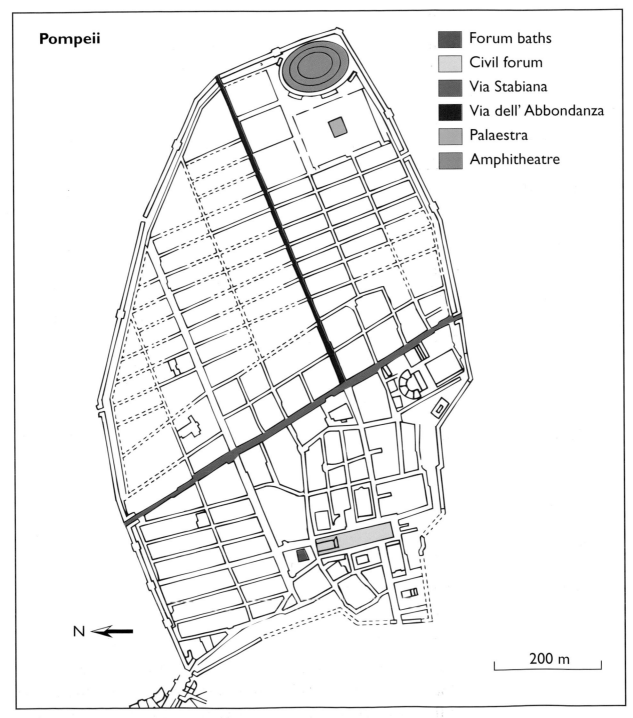

Pompeii

Forum baths
Civil forum
Via Stabiana
Via dell' Abbondanza
Palaestra
Amphitheatre

N

200 m

Glossary

aediles elected officials responsible for cleaning and repairing the streets, water and sanitation, organizing markets and the games in the amphitheatre

amphitheatre the great arena used for gladiatorial combats, animal fighting and chariot racing

apodyterium the dressing-room at the public baths

archaeologist a person who studies the past by looking at ancient ruins and remains

atrium the large entrance hall of a house. It was usually partly covered and partly open to the sky. Smaller rooms opened off it.

basilica the building used for meetings of lawyers and the hearing of lawsuits. It was also the place where businessmen met and made deals.

caldarium the hot room at the public baths

cock-fighting a fight between two birds as sport

colonnade a series of columns supporting a roof

duovirii the elected magistrates of the town. They were responsible for law and order.

forum a large open space in a Roman town. It was the social and business centre of the town. Important buildings like the basilica and temples to the gods were grouped round it. If a town had no amphitheatre, the forum was often used for games and parades.

frigidarium the cold room at the public baths

fuller's earth a fine clay mixed with water and used to clean cloth by trampling it underfoot

fullonica a workshop for cleaning and dyeing cloth and clothes

garum a strong-smelling sauce made from eggs and the fermented guts of fish

gladiator a slave or prisoner of war who was trained to fight as public entertainment. Most of them could only expect to die in combat. A few were able to gain their freedom because of their great success (in killing other gladiators).

impluvium a stone tank in the centre of the atrium. It collected the water that fell through the opening in the centre of the roof when it rained. It often had a well beside it.

lararium the small shrine where the household gods (or lares) were worshipped

macellum the main market in the town. All types of fresh food were sold here: meat, fish, fruit and vegetables. It also contained a place for changing money.

mosaic a pattern or picture made from small pieces of coloured glass, tiles or stone

palaestrum the gymnasium where young men went to get exercise, to train for athletic events and to swim

pergola a series of columns supporting a trellis over which plants can be grown

peristyle the garden of a house, usually surrounded by columns and a veranda. There were usually rooms opening on to the veranda, to take advantage of the light and the view into the garden.

potash a chemical used for bleaching

republic a country governed by an elected government rather than a king or queen

sundial an instrument that tells the time from the position of a shadow made by the sun

tepidarium the warm room at the public baths

thermopolium an inn where hot and cold wine and food were served. They often also provided entertainment and were used for gambling games.

triclinium the dining-room of a house. Larger houses often had more than one of these.

trident a spear with three points, like a fork

*I*ndex